Chocolate Overload!

SEASONAL BAKES MADE
WITH YOUR FAVOURITE TREATS

Jessie Bakes Cakes

1

Pop Press, an imprint of Ebury Publishing,
20 Vauxhall Bridge Road,
London SW1V 2SA

Pop Press is part of the Penguin Random House group of companies
whose addresses can be found at global.penguinrandomhouse.com

Text by Jessie Marsden-Urquhart © Penguin Random House 2024
Design by maru studio G.K.
Food photography by Jessie Marsden-Urquhart
Author photography by Stories by Chloe
Endpaper illustration by AnzhelikaP (Shutterstock)

Jessie Marsden-Urquhart has asserted her right to be identified as
the author of this work in accordance with the Copyright, Designs and
Patents Act 1988

First published by Ebury Press in 2024

www.penguin.co.uk

A CIP catalogue record for this book is available from
the British Library

ISBN 9781529915518

Colour origination by Altaimage Ltd, London
Printed and bound in Malaysia by Times Offset (M) Sdn Bhd

The authorised representative in the EEA is Penguin Random House
Ireland, Morrison Chambers, 32 Nassau Street, Dublin D02 YH68

MIX
Paper | Supporting
responsible forestry
FSC® C018179

Penguin Random House is committed to a sustainable future for
our business, our readers and our planet. This book is made from
Forest Stewardship Council® certified paper.

For all microwave instructions, use highest heat setting/full power.

introduction **4**

Brownies
& Blondies **7**

Cakes **27**

Cookies **43**

Cupcakes **63**

Slabs &
Sharing Boards **77**

index **94**
About the Author & Acknowledgements **96**

Introduction

Welcome to *Chocolate Overload* – my first ever cookbook!
Get ready to experience chocolate indulgence all year
round with this collection of seasonal recipes made using
your favourite chocolate treats.

In each chapter, you'll find chocolatey recipes that
celebrate Easter, Halloween and Christmas. Plus, I've
sprinkled in a few 'seasonal twist' ideas to include recipes
for other key moments, and with a simple decoration
tweak many of these bakes would work at any time of the
year – birthdays, dinner parties, BBQ's – take your pick!

From rich brownies to gooey cookies, sharing desserts
to decorative cupcakes, this cookbook covers all the
baking favourites with something for everyone. I've
carefully crafted each recipe to be no-fuss, using minimal
ingredients and simple equipment. So, whether you're
a seasoned baker or a complete novice in the kitchen,
I promise these delicious treats can be made and
enjoyed by all.

I hope this book brings you and your loved ones
as much joy as I had in creating it, and if you do
share your creations online, be sure to tag me at
@jessie.bakes.cakes on Instagram – I would love
to see them. Happy baking!

Brownies & Blondies

Dozen Egg Brownies

These Dozen Egg Brownies are fudgy, chocolatey and make an egg-cellent Easter treat! With three different flavours of chocolate eggs to choose from, which will be your favourite?

MAKES 12

- 150g unsalted butter, chopped
- 150g dark chocolate (70% cocoa solids), chopped
- 220g caster sugar
- 2 medium eggs, room temperature
- 150g self-raising flour
- 6 filled chocolate eggs
  (I use Cadbury Oreo Eggs, Cadbury Creme Eggs and Cadbury Caramel Eggs)

....

BAKING TIP
To halve the chocolate eggs more easily, run a sharp knife under boiling hot water before cutting.

Preheat the oven to 200°C/180°C fan. Then line a 20cm square baking tin with greaseproof paper.

Place the butter and dark chocolate in a heatproof bowl and melt in the microwave for 60–90 seconds, or set over a pan of simmering water until melted. Stir to combine and set aside to cool a little.

In a separate bowl, whisk the sugar and eggs together for 1 minute until pale and foamy.

Pour the cooled melted chocolate mixture into the whisked eggs and add the flour. Fold together to combine.

Transfer to the baking tin, spread out evenly and bake for 18 minutes. When ready, the brownies should look set on top and have a slight wobble underneath.

Meanwhile, cut each chocolate egg in half so you have 12 halves in total. As soon as the brownies are out of the oven and still warm, press the halved chocolate eggs into the top (3 across and 4 down).

Leave to cool completely (2 hours in the fridge or 4 hours at room temperature) before slicing into 12 and devouring.

Hot Cross Bun Brownies

Put a chocolatey twist on an Easter favourite with this tempting Hot Cross Bun Brownies recipe! Flavoured with cinnamon spice and studded with sultanas, these brownies are finished with a white chocolate orange cross.

MAKES 9

- 150g unsalted butter, chopped
- 150g dark chocolate (70% cocoa solids), chopped
- 220g caster sugar
- 2 medium eggs, room temperature
- 150g self-raising flour
- 1 tsp ground cinnamon
- 100g sultanas
- 50g orange-flavoured white chocolate (I use Terry's White Chocolate Orange), chopped

Preheat the oven to 200°C/180°C fan. Line a 20cm square baking tin with greaseproof paper.

Place the butter and dark chocolate in a heatproof bowl and melt in the microwave for 60–90 seconds, or set over a pan of simmering water until melted. Stir to combine and set aside to cool a little.

In a separate bowl, whisk the sugar and eggs together for 1 minute until pale in colour and foamy.

Pour the cooled melted chocolate mixture into the whisked eggs and add the flour and cinnamon. Fold together to combine. Gently stir in the sultanas.

Transfer to the baking tin, spread out evenly and bake for 18 minutes. When ready, the brownies should look set on top and have a slight wobble underneath. Leave to cool completely (2 hours in the fridge or 4 hours at room temperature).

To decorate, put the orange-flavoured white chocolate in a heatproof bowl and melt in the microwave for 60–90 seconds, or set over a pan of simmering water until melted. Transfer carefully to a piping bag. Snip off the tip and pipe three lines across and three lines down. Slice and enjoy!

Lemon & White Chocolate Bunny Blondies

If you're a fan of citrus flavours, you're in for a treat with these Lemon & White Chocolate Bunny Blondies! They're chewy around the edges, soft in the middle and decorated with adorable white chocolate bunnies for a very hoppy Easter finish.

MAKES 9

- 170g unsalted butter
- 250g light brown sugar
- 2 medium eggs, room temperature
- 1 tsp vanilla extract
- 180g self-raising flour
- zest of 1 lemon + juice of ½ lemon
- 50g white chocolate, melted
- 5-9 malt white chocolate bunnies (I use Mini Malteser Bunnies)

Preheat the oven to 190°C/170°C fan. Then line a 20cm square baking tin with greaseproof paper.

Place the butter in a large heatproof bowl and melt in the microwave for 30–60 seconds until it turns to liquid.

Add the sugar, eggs and vanilla extract to the melted butter and combine well. Fold in the flour until the mixture is smooth.

Add the zest of the whole lemon and the juice of half. Stir to combine.

Transfer to the tin and bake for 25 minutes. When ready, the blondies should look set on top and have a slight wobble underneath. Leave to cool completely (2 hours in the fridge or 4 hours at room temperature).

Drizzle over the melted white chocolate and slice into 9 blondies. To finish, either decorate with a handful of white chocolate bunnies or place one on top of each blondie if you have enough. Slice and devour!

Bubbling Cauldron Brownies

Grab your broomstick and whip up a batch of these Bubbling Cauldron Brownies. With a fudgy chocolate brownie cup and spooky cauldron decoration, they're sure to cast a spell on anyone who tastes them! Baking for a Halloween party? Double the ingredients to make a big batch of 24.

MAKES 12

Brownies
- 150g unsalted butter, chopped
- 150g dark chocolate (70% cocoa solids), chopped
- 220g caster sugar
- 2 medium eggs, room temperature
- 150g self-raising flour

Decoration
- 6 filled chocolate eggs (I use Cadbury Goo Heads)
- green food colouring
- 12 chocolate or pretzel sticks (I use Matchmakers)
- green and white edible balls
- edible eyes

Preheat the oven to 200°C/180°C fan and lightly grease a 12-hole cupcake tin with butter or cooking spray.

Place the butter and chocolate in a heatproof bowl and melt in the microwave for 60–90 seconds, or set over a pan of simmering water. Stir to combine and set aside to cool.

In a separate bowl, whisk the sugar and eggs for 1 minute until pale in colour and foamy.

Pour the cooled melted chocolate mixture into the eggs and add the flour. Fold to combine.

Divide the mixture evenly between the holes in the cupcake tin and bake for 12 minutes.

Meanwhile, chop each chocolate egg in half so you have 12 halves in total. Dab a toothpick in green food colouring and swirl it in the middle of each egg half to turn the filling green.

As soon as the brownie cups are out of the oven, press half a chocolate egg into the middle of each. Leave to cool completely (2 hours in the fridge or 4 hours at room temperature) and then use a knife to gently release the brownie cups from the tin.

Push a chocolate or pretzel stick 'cauldron stirrer' into each green egg filling. Then add the edible 'potion bubble' balls and the eyes for extra spook factor!

Cosmic Bat Brownies

These Cosmic Bat Brownies start with a dense and gooey brownie base, topped with rich chocolate ganache and decorated with chocolate button bats. Be warned ... they're sinfully rich, frightfully indulgent and will fly away in no time!

MAKES 12

Brownies
- 150g unsalted butter, chopped
- 150g dark chocolate (70% cocoa solids), chopped
- 220g caster sugar
- 2 medium eggs, room temperature
- 150g self-raising flour

Ganache
- 150g dark chocolate (70% cocoa solids), finely chopped
- 150g milk chocolate, finely chopped
- 300ml double cream

Decoration
- handful of chocolate buttons
- edible eyes
- Halloween sprinkles

Preheat the oven to 200°C/180°C fan and then line a 20cm square baking tin with greaseproof paper.

Place the butter and dark chocolate in a heatproof bowl and melt in the microwave for 60–90 seconds or set over a pan of simmering water until melted. Stir to combine and set aside to cool a little.

In a separate bowl, whisk the sugar and eggs together for one minute until pale in colour and foamy.

Pour the cooled melted chocolate mixture into the whisked eggs and add the flour. Fold to combine.

Transfer to the tin, spread out evenly and bake for 18 minutes. The brownies should look set on top and have a slight wobble underneath. Chill in the fridge for 1 hour.

Meanwhile, make the ganache by adding the dark chocolate, milk chocolate and double cream to a heatproof bowl. Microwave for 90 seconds, then let sit for 20 seconds before stirring until smooth. If the ganache splits, stir in a tablespoon of cream to bring it back together.

Pour the ganache over the chilled brownies and spread it out to the edges.

Stick half of the chocolate buttons over the ganache. Chop the remaining buttons in half and arrange them around the whole buttons so that they look like bat wings. Use a dab of leftover ganache to stick the eyes onto the buttons.

Fill in the empty spaces with Halloween sprinkles, then transfer to the fridge for 1 hour to set. Slice and dig in!

Trick-or-Treat Blondie Bars

Leftover trick-or-treat goodies? Bake them into a rich, buttery blondie for a scarily tasty treat! This recipe is super easy and versatile, just chuck in any leftover chocolates, sweets or biscuits to mix and match the flavours.

MAKES 9

- 170g salted butter
- 250g light brown sugar
- 2 medium eggs, room temperature
- 1 tsp vanilla extract
- 180g self-raising flour
- 200g leftover trick-or-treat goodies (I use M&M's, Candy Corns, fun size chocolate bars and mini Reese's Peanut Butter Cups)

Preheat the oven to 190°C/170°C fan. Then line a 20cm square baking tin with greaseproof paper.

Place the butter in a large heatproof bowl and melt in the microwave for 30–60 seconds.

Add the brown sugar, eggs and vanilla extract to the melted butter and combine well. Add the flour and fold to combine.

Chop up the trick-or-treat goodies and fold them into the mixture.

Transfer to the baking tin, spread out evenly and bake for 25 minutes. The blondies should look set on top and have a slight wobble underneath when ready.

Leave to cool completely (2 hours in the fridge or 4 hours at room temperature), then slice and enjoy!

BAKING TIP
For a decorative finish, press a handful of goodies into the top of the blondies before baking.

Rudolph Brownies

These adorable red-nosed Rudolph Brownies are sure to make you feel festive. The simple and easy reindeer decoration is perfect for getting little ones involved, and I recommend listening to 'Run Rudolph Run' during baking for even more festive feels!

MAKES 12

- 150g unsalted butter, chopped
- 150g dark chocolate (70% cocoa solids), chopped
- 220g caster sugar
- 2 medium eggs, room temperature
- 150g self-raising flour
- icing pen
- 24 edible eyes
- 24 mini pretzels
- 12 red chocolate beans (I use M&M's)

Preheat the oven to 200°C/180°C fan and line a 20cm square baking tin with greaseproof paper.

Place the butter and dark chocolate in a heatproof bowl and melt in the microwave for 60–90 seconds, or set over a pan of simmering water until melted. Stir to combine and set aside to cool a little.

In a separate bowl, whisk the sugar and eggs together for 1 minute until pale and foamy.

Pour the cooled melted chocolate mixture into the whisked eggs and add the flour. Fold to combine.

Transfer to the baking tin, spread out evenly and bake for 18 minutes. When ready, the brownies should be set on top with a slight wobble underneath. Leave to cool completely (2 hours in the fridge or 4 hours at room temperature), then slice into 12.

To create the Rudolph faces, use the icing pen to stick the eyes, pretzels and red chocolate beans on top of the brownies.

Red Velvet Santa Hat Blondies

Santa is definitely coming to town for these Red Velvet Santa Hat Blondies! They're flavoured with rich cocoa and sweet vanilla, with chunks of creamy white chocolate dotted throughout.

MAKES 8

Red Velvet Blondies
- 200g unsalted butter
- 300g light brown sugar
- 1 tsp vanilla extract
- ½ tsp white wine vinegar
- 3 medium eggs, room temperature
- 1 tsp red food colouring (oil or gel-based works best)
- 220g self-raising flour
- 1½ tbsp cocoa powder
- 100g white chocolate, chopped into chunks

Decoration
- 50g white chocolate, melted
- 8 coated chocolate snowballs (I use Cadbury Mini Snow Balls)
- icing sugar, for dusting

....

BAKING TIP

For the bobble, you can use either coated chocolate snowballs, white chocolate buttons or mini marshmallows.

Preheat the oven to 190°C/170°C fan. Then line a 20cm square baking tin with greaseproof paper.

Place the butter in a large heatproof bowl and melt in the microwave for 30–60 seconds until it turns to liquid.

Add the brown sugar, vanilla extract, white wine vinegar and eggs to the bowl and mix until well combined.

Stir in the red food colouring to dye the mixture bright red (the brighter the better!).

Sift in the flour and cocoa powder. Fold to combine. Then carefully stir in the white chocolate chunks.

Transfer to the baking tin, spread out evenly and bake for 35 minutes. When ready, the blondies should be set on top with a slight wobble underneath. Leave to cool completely in the tin (2 hours in the fridge or 4 hours at room temperature).

Once cool, slice the blondies down the middle, then slice each half in a zigzag pattern to make triangle shapes (4 in each half; 8 in total).

To decorate, pipe the melted white chocolate along the bottom of each triangle and stick a snowball at the peak at the top of each. Finish with a dusting of icing sugar.

Try this seasonal twist

For a Valentine's treat, cut the blondies into squares, drizzle with white chocolate and decorate with heart sprinkles.

Snowball Brownies

Filled with crunchy milk chocolate snowballs and dusted with icing sugar for a wintery finish, these Snowball Brownies are perfect for any occasion – from Christmas parties to cosy nights in with a hot chocolate.

MAKES 9

- 150g unsalted butter, chopped
- 150g dark chocolate (70% cocoa solids), chopped
- 220g caster sugar
- 2 medium eggs, room temperature
- 150g self-raising flour
- 160g coated chocolate snowballs (I use Cadbury Mini SnowBalls)
- icing sugar, for dusting

Preheat the oven to 200°C/180°C fan. Then line a 20cm square baking tin with greaseproof paper.

Place the butter and dark chocolate in a heatproof bowl and melt in the microwave for 60–90 seconds, or set over a pan of simmering water until melted. Stir to combine and set aside to cool a little.

In a separate bowl, whisk the caster sugar and eggs together for 1 minute until pale in colour and foamy.

Pour the cooled melted chocolate mixture into the whisked eggs and add the flour. Fold together to combine.

Bash the chocolate snowballs with a rolling pin to break them up, then fold into the brownie mixture.

Transfer to the baking tin, spread out evenly and bake for 18 minutes. When ready, the brownies should be set on top with a slight wobble underneath. Leave to cool completely in the tin (2 hours in the fridge or 4 hours at room temperature).

Dust with icing sugar, then slice and share.

Cakes

Carrot Patch Cake

Strawberry carrots, walnut 'soil' and white chocolate bunnies decorate this delicious Carrot Patch Cake with white chocolate cream cheese frosting. It's an Easter showstopper that is sure to impress your friends and family!

SERVES 12

Cake
- 300g light brown sugar
- 4 medium eggs, room temperature
- 300ml sunflower oil
- 2 tsp vanilla extract
- 300g self-raising flour
- 2 tsp mixed spice
- zest of 1 large orange
- 200g carrots, grated
- 100g walnuts, chopped

Frosting
- 125g salted butter, room temperature
- 200g icing sugar
- 125g full-fat cream cheese, use cold from the fridge
- 60g white chocolate, melted and cooled

Decoration
- orange oil-based food colouring
- 50g white chocolate, melted
- 4 strawberries
- 50g walnuts
- 4 malt white chocolate bunnies (I use Mini Malteser Bunnies)

Preheat the oven to 180°C/160°C fan. Grease and line the base of a 30 x 20cm baking tin with greaseproof paper.

In a large bowl, mix the brown sugar, eggs, sunflower oil and vanilla extract together. In a separate bowl, stir the flour, mixed spice and orange zest together. Add to the wet ingredients and fold together until the mixture is smooth and combined. Then fold in the grated carrot and chopped walnuts.

Transfer to the tin, spread out evenly and bake for 45–50 minutes until the sponge is risen and springy to the touch. Leave to cool completely.

To make the frosting, first beat the butter until soft and smooth. Sift in the icing sugar and beat again until combined. Add the cold cream cheese and gently fold in. Pour in the melted white chocolate and stir to combine, then spread the frosting on top of the cake, using the back of a spoon to make a swirly pattern.

To make the strawberry 'carrots', stir a few drops of orange food colouring into the melted white chocolate. Dip the strawberries first, then drizzle over any leftover chocolate. Place in the fridge to set.

Meanwhile, blitz the walnuts in a blender or food processor until they reach a soil-like texture. Spoon the walnut soil on top of the frosting in patches, then place the strawberry carrots on top. Finish by decorating with the white chocolate bunnies, then slice and feast!

Try this seasonal twist

For a Mother's Day treat, swap the decorations for whole walnuts and edible flowers.

Chocolate Simnel Cake

Inspired by the traditional Easter recipe, this Chocolate Simnel Cake incorporates rich, chocolate flavours in every bite. From the spiced chocolate chip sponge to the golden chocolate egg decorations, even the most dedicated chocoholics will be satisfied with this indulgent recipe!

SERVES 10

Cake
- 500g white marzipan
- 200g unsalted butter, room temperature
- 200g light brown sugar
- 180g self-raising flour
- 30g cocoa powder
- 2 tsp mixed spice
- 3 medium eggs, room temperature, beaten
- 3 tbsp milk
- 200g dark chocolate chips

Ganache
- 100g dark chocolate (70% cocoa solids), finely chopped
- 100ml double cream

Decoration
- 11 golden chocolate eggs, approx 60g weight in total (I use Galaxy Golden Eggs)

Preheat the oven to 170°C/150°C fan. Grease and line the base of a 20cm round cake tin with greaseproof paper.

Sandwich the marzipan between two sheets of greaseproof paper and roll it out to roughly 1cm thickness. Cut out a 20cm circle of marzipan (you can use the cake tin as a guide). Roll the leftover marzipan into 11 small balls and use your thumb to make a dip in the top of each ball. Set aside.

In a large bowl, cream the butter and brown sugar together until light and fluffy.

In a separate bowl, stir the flour, cocoa powder and mixed spice together.

Add one-third of the beaten eggs and one-third of the dry ingredients into the butter mixture and beat until combined. Repeat until all the ingredients are combined and the cake mixture is smooth.

Fold in the milk and dark chocolate chips until evenly distributed through the mixture.

Transfer half of the cake mixture to the cake tin and spread it out evenly. Place the 20cm circle of marzipan on top, followed by the rest of the cake mixture.

Bake for 55–60 minutes until risen and springy to the touch (a toothpick inserted into the middle should come out clean). Leave to cool completely.

To make the ganache, place the chopped chocolate and double cream in a heatproof bowl and microwave for 45 seconds. Leave to sit for 20 seconds, then stir to make a smooth ganache. If the ganache splits, stir in an extra tablespoon of cream to bring it back together.

Pour the ganache on top of the cake and spread it out evenly to the edges. Arrange the marzipan balls around the outside. Use a dab of leftover ganache to stick a golden egg in the middle of each marzipan ball. Slice and serve!

31

Hot Cross Mug Cake

Prep, bake and enjoy this delicious Hot Cross Mug Cake in less than five minutes! Studded with sultanas and filled with mini chocolate orange eggs, it's perfect for satisfying your sweet cravings over the Easter season.

SERVES 1

- 3 tbsp self-raising flour
- 1 tbsp light brown sugar
- ½ tsp ground cinnamon, plus extra for dusting
- ½ tsp vanilla extract
- 1 tbsp sunflower oil
- 2 tbsp milk
- 10g raisins
- 5 chocolate orange eggs (I use Terry's Chocolate Orange Mini Eggs)

Stir the flour, brown sugar and ground cinnamon together in a medium-sized microwaveable mug.

Mix in the vanilla extract, sunflower oil and milk until smooth. Stir in the raisins and chocolate orange eggs.

Microwave on full power for approximately 90 seconds (the cooking time may differ by 10–20 seconds, depending on how powerful your microwave is). The mug cake is ready when it has risen and started to pull away from the sides.

To decorate, cut two strips of kitchen paper and lay them on top of the mug cake in a cross. Dust with ground cinnamon, then carefully lift off the strips to reveal the cross. Grab a spoon and get stuck in!

Monster Mash Loaf Cake

This vanilla and chocolate Monster Mash Loaf Cake screams spooky season! Experiment with different food colourings and mix and match different Halloween sprinkles for a spooktacular finish.

SERVES 10

Cake
- 300g unsalted butter, room temperature
- 300g caster sugar
- 4 medium eggs, room temperature
- 300g self-raising flour
- 2 tbsp milk
- purple, green and orange food colourings (oil or gel-based work best)

Icing
- 200g icing sugar
- 50g cocoa powder
- 6–8 tbsp milk

Decoration
- edible eyes
- Halloween sprinkles

Preheat the oven to 180°C/160°C fan and line a 900g loaf tin with greaseproof paper.

Cream the butter and caster sugar together until light and fluffy. Mix in the eggs one at a time along with 1 tablespoon of the flour.

Next, fold in the remaining flour, add the milk and stir until smooth and combined.

Divide the mixture equally between three bowls and dye each a different colour using the food colourings.

Drop large spoonfuls of the cake mixtures into the loaf tin, alternating between the different colours. Give the tin a final shake to level out the mixture.

Bake for 60–65 minutes until risen and springy to the touch (a toothpick inserted into the middle should come out clean). Leave to cool completely.

To make the icing, mix all the ingredients together in a bowl until smooth. Pour the icing over the cake letting it drip down the sides.

Finish by decorating with edible eyes and Halloween sprinkles to add some spook. Slice and enjoy!

Halloween Party Cake

Hosting a Halloween party? This too-cute-to-spook traybake is the perfect centrepiece for your table spread. The fluffy vanilla sponge is studded with colourful chocolate beans, topped with sweet buttercream and decorated with white chocolate ghosts. Feel free to customise the cake with a personalised chocolate message!

SERVES 15+

Cake
- 350g unsalted butter, room temperature
- 350g white caster sugar
- 2 tsp vanilla extract
- 4 medium eggs, room temperature
- 350g self raising flour
- 200g chocolate beans (I used M&Ms for bright pops of colour)

Buttercream
- 400g salted butter, room temperature
- 750g icing sugar
- 2 tbsp milk
- Purple food colouring

Decoration
- 200g white chocolate, melted
- Chocolate writing icing

Preheat the oven to 160°C fan / 180°C conventional. Grease and line a 30x20cm traybake tin with greaseproof paper.

Cream the butter, sugar and vanilla together in a large bowl until light and fluffy. Mix in the eggs one at a time with 1 tablespoon of flour.

Add the remaining flour and fold in until smooth and combined. Transfer to the baking tin, spread out evenly, and then scatter the chocolate beans on top.

Bake for 45-50 minutes until risen and springy to the touch (a toothpick inserted into the middle should come out clean). Leave to cool completely.

To make the buttercream, first beat the butter until soft and smooth. Sift in the icing sugar and add the milk. Beat well until smooth and combined. Mix in a few drops of purple colouring to dye the buttercream a lilac shade.

Spread the buttercream over the cake and then use the chocolate writing icing to write your message in the middle (get creative!).

Next dot teaspoons of melted white chocolate around the top of the cake and use the back of the spoon to spread them into ghost shapes. Add the ghosts' eyes and mouths using the chocolate writing icing.

Chill in the fridge for 20 minutes to set the chocolate, then slice and devour!

Chocolate Orange Wreath Cake

Offering a delicious blend of zesty orange and rich chocolate flavours, this Chocolate Orange Wreath Cake is a fabulously festive centrepiece for your Christmas table. Plus, it has wow-factor but is surprisingly easy to make!

SERVES 10

Cake
- 375g golden caster sugar
- 300g self-raising flour
- 75g cocoa powder
- 150ml vegetable oil
- 450ml milk
- 3 medium eggs, room temperature, beaten
- zest and juice of 1 orange

Ganache
- 100g dark chocolate (70% cocoa solids), finely chopped
- 100ml double cream

Decoration
- chocolate orange segments (I use Terry's Chocolate Orange)
- Christmas sprinkles
- fresh rosemary sprigs
- edible gold spray

Preheat the oven to 180°C/160°C fan. Grease and line the base and sides of a 23cm round cake tin with greaseproof paper.

In a large bowl, stir the sugar, flour and cocoa powder together. Add the vegetable oil, milk, beaten eggs and the orange zest and juice. Whisk together to make a smooth chocolate cake mixture.

Transfer to the cake tin, spreading out evenly, then bake for 40–45 minutes until risen and springy to the touch. Leave to cool completely.

To make the ganache, put the chopped chocolate and double cream in a heatproof bowl and microwave for 45 seconds. Leave to sit for 20 seconds, then stir until smooth. If the ganache splits, stir in an extra tablespoon of cream to bring it back together.

Pour the ganache over the top of the cake, letting it drip down the sides. Use the back of a spoon to make a swirl or two on top.

Arrange the chocolate orange segments around the outside of the top of the cake to create a wreath.

Decorate with Christmas sprinkles, rosemary sprigs and edible gold spray to add some shimmer. Slice and share!

Rudolph Malted Chocolate Mug Cake

With a rich malt chocolate sponge and cute Rudolph decoration, this five-minute mug cake is sure to put a smile on your face. Perfect for a quick sweet treat while you cosy down with a Christmas movie!

SERVES 1

Cake
- 3 tbsp self-raising flour
- ½ tbsp cocoa powder
- ½ tbsp malted hot chocolate powder
- 1 tbsp caster sugar
- 1 tsp sunflower oil
- 3 tbsp milk
- 1 tbsp boiling water
- 5 malt chocolate balls (I use Maltesers)

Toppings
- whipped cream
- malt chocolate reindeer (I use Mini Malteser Reindeer)
- red chocolate beans (I use M&M's)

Mix all the mug cake ingredients together in a medium-sized microwavable mug.

Microwave on full power for approximately 90 seconds (the cooking time may differ by 10–20 seconds, depending on how powerful your microwave is). The mug cake is ready when it has risen and started to pull away from the sides.

Top with whipped cream, a malt chocolate reindeer and red chocolate beans. Best enjoyed straightaway!

Cookies

Bunny Hug Biscuits

Buttery, zesty and oh-so-sweet – these lemon-flavoured Bunny Hug Biscuits are a delicious Easter treat. You only need five ingredients and can use an upside-down gingerbread man cutter to create the bunny shape. Easy-peasy lemon squeezy!

MAKES 15

- 100g unsalted butter, room temperature
- 50g caster sugar
- 200g plain flour, plus extra for dusting
- zest of 1 lemon
- 15 mini chocolate eggs (I use Cadbury Mini Eggs)

Preheat the oven to 180°C/160°C fan and line a baking sheet with greaseproof paper.

Cream the butter and sugar together in a bowl until light and fluffy.

Add the flour and lemon zest and with your hands work the mixture into a dough. If it's a little dry, add a drop of water. Wrap in clingfilm and chill in the fridge for 30 minutes.

Lightly dust a work surface and rolling pin with flour, then roll the dough out to ½cm thickness. Use a gingerbread man cutter to stamp out shapes (you will need to gather the scraps and reroll them to make all 15 biscuits).

Place the shapes upside down on the baking sheet, so what would have been the legs of each man become the bunny ears. Pinch the top of the ears so they're less rounded and more pointed. Press a mini chocolate egg in the middle of each bunny and carefully shape the arms around them. With a toothpick, make deep holes for the eyes and noses.

Chill in the fridge for another 30 minutes to firm up the dough (this will help the bunnies keep their shape when baking).

Bake for 10 minutes until golden around the edges. Leave to cool, pop the kettle on and enjoy with a cup of tea.

Salted Caramel Egg Cookies

With crisp edges and an ultra-fudgy centre, these Salted Caramel Egg Cookies are the perfect balance of sweet and salty. Ideal for those craving a rich and indulgent chocolatey treat over Easter!

MAKES 10

- 75g unsalted butter, chopped
- 150g dark chocolate (70% cocoa solids), chopped
- 100g caster sugar
- 100g light brown sugar
- 2 medium eggs, room temperature
- 150g self-raising flour
- 5 caramel-filled chocolate eggs (I use Cadbury Caramel Eggs)
- flaky sea salt, for sprinkling

Place the butter and dark chocolate in a heatproof bowl and melt in the microwave for 60–90 seconds, or set over a pan of simmering water until melted. Stir to combine and set aside to cool a little.

In a separate bowl, whisk the two sugars and eggs together until thick and foamy.

Pour in the cooled melted chocolate mixture and add the flour. Fold to combine.

Cover the bowl with clingfilm and chill in the fridge for 15 minutes to firm up.

Meanwhile, preheat the oven to 200°C/180°C fan and line two large baking sheets with greaseproof paper. Drop heaped tablespoons of the mixture onto the baking sheets, leaving 5cm space between each so the cookies have room to spread out. You should be able to fit 10 cookies in total (5 on each baking sheet).

Bake for 10 minutes until firm around the edges and set on top. Meanwhile, carefully halve the caramel eggs using a sharp knife.

As soon as the cookies are out of the oven, press half a caramel egg into the middle of each. Leave to cool on the baking sheets for 20 minutes, then sprinkle with flaky sea salt and enjoy!

Try this seasonal twist

NO.1 DAD

Swap the caramel eggs for colourful chocolate letters to spell out a thoughtful Father's Day message.

Egg Hunt Cookie Bars

Put all your favourite chocolate mini eggs in one basket ... or in the case of this recipe, a soft and gooey Egg Hunt Cookie Bar! From mixing bowl to first bite in less than an hour, there's no excuse not to experiment and find your favourite flavour.

MAKES 12

- 150g unsalted butter
- 100g caster sugar
- 150g light brown sugar
- 1 medium egg, room temperature
- 1 medium egg yolk, room temperature
- 1 tsp vanilla extract
- 275g self-raising flour
- ½ tsp salt
- 300g mini chocolate eggs (I use a mix of Cadbury Mini Eggs, Galaxy Golden Eggs, Milkybar Mini Eggs and Smarties Mini Eggs)

Preheat the oven to 200°C/180°C fan. Then line a 20cm square baking tin with greaseproof paper.

Place the butter in a large heatproof bowl and melt in the microwave for 30–60 seconds until it turns to liquid.

Mix in the two sugars, the egg, egg yolk and vanilla extract until combined. Fold in the flour and salt to make a thick cookie dough.

Fold 250g of the mini chocolate eggs into the dough, then press out into the baking tin. Use a rolling pin to bash the remaining eggs into pieces and scatter them over the top.

Bake for 18–20 minutes. The cookie bars should look golden and set on top, with a slight wobble underneath.

Leave to cool in the baking tin for 30 minutes, then slice into 12 bars and serve!

....

BAKING TIP
Cookie bars will continue to cook as they cool down, so it's best to underbake them. If in doubt, take them out!

Cookies & Scream Bars

In need of a last-minute Halloween treat? Give these quick and easy Cookies & Scream Bars a go! The buttery cookie dough is layered with crunchy cookies & cream biscuits. If you can find them, use biscuits with an orange-coloured cream for a spooky pop of colour!

MAKES 12

- 150g unsalted butter
- 100g caster sugar
- 150g light brown sugar
- 1 medium egg, room temperature
- 1 medium egg yolk, room temperature
- 2 tsp vanilla extract
- 275g self-raising flour
- ½ tsp salt
- 300g cookies & cream biscuits with orange-coloured cream (I use Halloween Oreos)

Preheat the oven to 200°C/180°C fan. Then line a 20cm square baking tin with greaseproof paper.

Place the butter in a large heatproof bowl and melt in the microwave for 30–60 seconds until it turns to liquid.

Mix in the two sugars, the egg, egg yolk and vanilla extract until combined. Fold in the flour and salt to make a thick cookie dough.

Press half of the cookie dough into the baking tin and top with a layer of cookies & cream biscuits. Top with the remaining cookie dough and press it out to the edges of the tin to conceal the biscuits underneath.

Use a rolling pin to crush up the remaining biscuits and scatter them over the top.

Bake for 18–20 minutes. The cookie bars should look golden and set on top, with a slight wobble underneath.

Leave to cool in the baking tin for 30 minutes, then slice into 12 bars and enjoy!

Try this seasonal twist

For a Thanksgiving Day treat, swap the biscuits for pecans, dark chocolate and caramelised white chocolate.

Maple Mummy Cookies

Sink your teeth into these frightfully delicious Maple Mummy Cookies! With a soft and chewy centre and perfectly crisp edges, these cookies are flavoured with sweet maple syrup and spicy cinnamon. Plus, it couldn't be easier to mummify the cookies using melted white chocolate and chocolate beans.

MAKES 15

- 160g unsalted butter, room temperature
- 100g caster sugar
- 150g light brown sugar
- 1 medium egg, room temperature
- 2 tsp maple syrup
- 250g self-raising flour
- 1 tsp ground cinnamon
- ½ tsp salt
- 100g white chocolate, chopped
- 100g chocolate beans (I use M&M's)

....

BAKING TIP
Want to prep ahead? You can wrap and freeze the rolled cookie dough balls for up to two months. Then bake from frozen at the same temperature for 14 minutes.

Preheat the oven to 200°C/180°C fan and then line two large baking sheets with greaseproof paper.

Cream the butter and two sugars together in a large mixing bowl. Stir in the egg and maple syrup until combined.

Fold in the flour, cinnamon and salt to make a thick cookie dough.

Scoop up heaped tablespoons of cookie dough and roll into balls. Repeat until all the dough is used up, making 15 balls in total. Place the balls on the baking sheets leaving 5cm space between each so they have room to spread out. Depending on the size of your baking sheets, you may need to bake the cookies in batches.

Bake for 10 minutes until firm around the outside edges but still pale in the middle. Leave the cookies to cool completely on the baking sheets.

Melt the white chocolate in a heatproof bowl in the microwave in 30 second blasts, or set over a pan of simmering water until melted.

Drizzle the white chocolate over the cookies, then add two chocolate beans for the mummy's eyes.

Try this seasonal twist

Swap the spiderweb decoration for chocolate stars and edible gold dusting for a dazzling Bonfire Night treat.

S'mores Spiderweb Cookies

Draped in a melted marshmallow web, these S'mores Spiderweb Cookies are filled with milk chocolate buttons, biscuit chunks and chewy marshmallows. Spooky has never tasted so good!

MAKES 15

- 150g unsalted butter, room temperature
- 100g caster sugar
- 150g light brown sugar
- 1 medium egg, room temperature
- 200g self-raising flour
- 50g cocoa powder
- 50g milk chocolate buttons, chopped into chunks
- 50g digestive biscuits, chopped into chunks
- 100g white mini marshmallows
- edible eyes

....

BAKING TIP
If the melted marshmallow becomes too sticky and is difficult to work with, just pop it back in the microwave for another 10 seconds.

Preheat the oven to 200°C/180°C fan and then line two large baking sheets with greaseproof paper.

Cream the butter and two sugars together in a large mixing bowl until well combined. Then mix in the egg. Then add the flour and cocoa powder and fold everything together to make a thick chocolate cookie dough.

Fold in the chocolate buttons, biscuit chunks and 30g of the mini marshmallows.

Scoop up heaped tablespoons of dough and roll into balls. Repeat until all the dough is used – 15 balls in total. Place the balls on the baking sheets, leaving 8cm space between each so they have room to spread out.

Bake for 8–10 minutes until firm around the edges then leave the cookies to cool.

Place the remaining marshmallows in a heatproof bowl and microwave for 30-seconds until melted and puffed up. If cool enough to touch, using your fingertips, grab a small amount and pull it apart to create a spiderweb effect. Drape the web over a cookie, wrapping it under the bottom. Repeat until all the cookies are covered in webs.

Decorate with edible eyes to bring the spiders to life, then tuck in and devour!

Cookies
for Santa

Studded with festive chocolate beans, these soft and chewy Christmas cookies are the perfect snack to bake for Santa. Best served by the fire with a glass of milk for dunking!

MAKES 14

- 150g unsalted butter, melted
- 100g caster sugar
- 150g light brown sugar
- 1 medium egg, room temperature
- 1 medium egg yolk, room temperature
- 1 tsp vanilla extract
- 275g self-raising flour
- ½ tsp salt
- 150g red, green and white chocolate beans (I use Christmas M&M's)

BAKING TIP
When baking the cookies in batches, keep the rolled cookie dough balls in the fridge so they don't get too soft.

Mix the melted butter and two sugars together in a large bowl.

Add the egg, egg yolk and vanilla extract and mix until combined. Add the flour and salt and fold together to make a cookie dough. Fold in 120g of the chocolate beans, reserving the remaining beans for decorating later.

Cover the bowl with clingfilm and chill in the fridge for 4 hours or overnight; the longer it chills, the better the texture and flavour.

Once the chill time is up, preheat the oven to 200°C/180°C fan and line two large baking sheets with greaseproof paper.

Allow the cookie dough to soften at room temperature for 20 minutes, then scoop up a heaped tablespoon of dough and roll into a ball. Repeat until all the dough is used up, you should be able to make 14 in total. Place the balls on the baking sheets 8cm apart, so they have room to spread as they bake.

Bake for 10 minutes until golden around the edges but the middles are still pale and soft.

As soon as the cookies are out of the oven, press the remaining chocolate beans into the top of each cookie to decorate.

Leave to cool on the baking sheets for at least 20 minutes. Serve with a glass of milk!

57

Linzer Love Cookies, Actually

To me, these cookies are perfect! Chocolate hazelnut spread is sandwiched between two crunchy chocolate biscuits and dusted with icing sugar for a festive finish. Use a variety of cutters to make different shapes and serve with a hot cup of tea for dunking.

MAKES 20

- 120g unsalted butter, room temperature
- 120g caster sugar
- 1 medium egg, room temperature
- 200g plain flour, plus extra for dusting
- 30g cocoa powder
- 60g ground almonds
- 150g chocolate hazelnut spread
- icing sugar, for dusting

In a large bowl, cream the butter and caster sugar together until light and fluffy. Add the egg and mix until combined.

In a separate bowl, stir the flour, cocoa powder and ground almonds together. Add to the butter mixture and combine until a dough is formed. Wrap in clingfilm and chill in the fridge for 30 minutes.

Lightly dust a work surface with flour and roll the dough out to roughly ½cm thickness. Use a 5cm fluted round cookie cutter to stamp out shapes. You will need to gather the scraps and reroll the dough to make 40 circles.

Use a variety of small cutters to stamp out the middle of half of the circles.

Carefully transfer to two lined baking sheets and chill in the fridge for 20 minutes.

Meanwhile, preheat the oven to 180°C/160°C fan. Bake the cookies for 8 minutes, then leave to cool completely.

Spread a teaspoon of chocolate hazelnut spread onto each of the cookies that doesn't have a shape cut out in the middle.

Dust icing sugar over the cookies that do have shapes cut out, then sandwich those over the chocolate hazelnut spread cookies.

Snowman Puddle Peanut Butter Cookies

Crisp and chewy peanut butter cookies make a delicious base for these adorable snowman puddles. The decoration couldn't be easier and it's a wonderful opportunity to get little ones involved in the kitchen. The messier the design, the more realistic the snowman puddles become!

MAKES 12

Cookies
- 200g smooth peanut butter
- 150g light brown sugar
- 1 medium egg, room temperature
- 1 tsp vanilla extract
- 1 tsp baking powder

Decoration
- 6 white marshmallows
- 200g white chocolate, melted
- 12 small peanut butter cups (I use Reese's Mini Cups)
- 6 chocolate or pretzel sticks (I use Matchmakers)
- edible gold balls
- chocolate writing icing
- orange strand sprinkles

Preheat the oven to 200°C/180°C fan and then line two large baking sheets with greaseproof paper.

Mix the peanut butter, brown sugar, egg, vanilla extract and baking powder together in a mixing bowl.

Drop 12 heaped teaspoons of the mixture onto the baking sheets, leaving 5cm space between each so they have room to spread out as they bake.

Bake for 8 minutes until golden and firm, then leave to cool completely.

To decorate, use scissors to cut each marshmallow in half widthways and place one half on top of each cookie.

Spoon the melted white chocolate on top of the marshmallows halves to make a melted snowman 'puddle'.

Add a peanut butter cup at an angle for each snowman's hat. Break up the chocolate or pretzel sticks and add two for the snowman's arms. Add two edible gold balls to each for the buttons.

Finish by using the chocolate writing icing to add two dots for the eyes and an orange strand sprinkle for the carrot nose.

Cupcakes

Easter Nest Cupcakes

Treat your friends and family to these eggs-tra special Easter Nest Cupcakes. With flavours of vanilla, white chocolate and toasted coconut, these cupcakes taste as delightful as they look!

MAKES 12

Cupcakes
- 180g unsalted butter, room temperature
- 180g caster sugar
- 2 medium eggs, room temperature
- 180g self-raising flour
- 1 tsp vanilla extract
- 2 tbsp milk

Buttercream
- 100g white chocolate, chopped
- 200g unsalted butter, room temperature
- 400g icing sugar

Decoration
- 100g toasted coconut flakes
- 200g mini chocolate eggs (I use Cadbury Mini Eggs)

Preheat the oven to 180°C/160°C fan and line a 12-hole cupcake tin with 12 paper cases.

Cream the butter and caster sugar together in a large bowl until light and fluffy. Beat in the eggs one at a time. Then fold in the flour, vanilla extract and milk to make a smooth cake mixture.

Divide the mixture evenly between the cases, filling each three-quarters full. Bake for 18–20 minutes until risen and springy to the touch (a toothpick inserted into the middle should come out clean). Leave to cool on a wire rack.

To make the buttercream, first melt the white chocolate in a heatproof bowl in the microwave in 30-second blasts, or set over a pan of simmering water until melted.

In a separate bowl, beat the butter until soft and pale in colour. Sift in the icing sugar and beat together until combined. Fold in the melted white chocolate.

Spread or pipe some buttercream on top of each cupcake. Then stick the coconut flakes into the buttercream to create a nest. Finish by placing 3 chocolate eggs in the middle of each nest.

Cracked Egg Chocolate Cupcakes

Decorated with an oozing chocolate egg, these cupcakes have an extra mini egg baked into the sponge and are topped with swirls of silky chocolate buttercream. Pure chocolate overload!

MAKES 12

Cupcakes
- 12 mini filled chocolate eggs (I use Cadbury Mini Creme Eggs)
- 180g unsalted butter, room temperature
- 180g caster sugar
- 2 medium eggs, room temperature
- 150g self-raising flour
- 30g cocoa powder

Buttercream
- 200g salted butter, room temperature
- 350g icing sugar
- 50g cocoa powder
- 2 tbsp boiling water

Decoration
- 6 filled chocolate eggs (I use Cadbury Creme Eggs)

Place the mini chocolate eggs in the freezer for at least an hour before starting the recipe.

Preheat the oven to 180°C/160°C fan and line a 12-hole cupcake tin with 12 paper cases.

Cream the butter and caster sugar together in a large bowl until light and fluffy. Beat in the eggs one at a time. Then fold in the flour and cocoa powder to make a smooth chocolate cake mixture.

Fill each case with a thin layer of mixture. Unwrap the frozen mini chocolate eggs and place one upright in the middle of each case. Spoon more mixture on top to conceal the eggs, filling each case three-quarters full.

Bake for 20–22 minutes until risen and springy to the touch. Leave to cool on a wire rack.

To make the buttercream, beat the butter in a bowl until soft and pale in colour. Sift in the icing sugar and beat until combined. Beat in the cocoa powder and boiling water to make a smooth and creamy chocolate buttercream.

Spread or pipe tall swirls of buttercream on top of each cupcake.

Use a sharp knife to halve the full-sized chocolate eggs so you have 12 halves in total. Top each cupcake with half an egg, letting the filling ooze out onto the buttercream. Enjoy!

Wicked Witch Cupcakes

Bite into these Wicked Witch Cupcakes to uncover flavours of sweet apple, spicy cinnamon and a surprise peanut butter chocolate bean centre. This recipe is all treats, no tricks!

MAKES 12

Cupcakes
- 180g unsalted butter, room temperature
- 180g caster sugar
- 2 medium eggs, room temperature
- 180g self-raising flour
- 1 tsp ground cinnamon
- 1 eating apple, peeled, cored and chopped into small chunks
- 60g peanut butter chocolate beans (I use Reese's Pieces)

Buttercream
- 200g unsalted butter, room temperature
- 400g icing sugar
- orange food colouring (oil or gel-based works best)

Decoration
- 6 cookies & cream biscuits (I use Oreos)
- 12 milk chocolate drops (I use Hershey's)

Preheat the oven to 180°C/160°C fan and line a 12-hole cupcake tin with 12 paper cases.

Cream the butter and sugar together until light and fluffy. Beat in the eggs one at a time. Then fold in the flour and cinnamon to make a smooth cake mixture. Fold through the apple chunks.

Divide the mixture evenly between the cases, filling each three-quarters full.

Bake for 20–22 minutes until risen and springy to the touch (a toothpick inserted into the middle should come out clean). Leave to cool completely on a wire rack.

Use a teaspoon to scoop out the middle of each cupcake and fill with peanut butter chocolate beans.

To make the buttercream, beat the butter until soft and pale in colour. Sift in the icing sugar in two stages, beating as you go, then mix in a few drops of orange food colouring. Transfer to a piping bag fitted with an open-star nozzle, and pipe buttercream swirls on each cupcake.

To decorate, separate the cookies & cream biscuits and remove the cream filling. Pipe a dot of buttercream on each biscuit and place a chocolate drop on top. You should now have 12 witch hats. Place a witch's hat on top of each cupcake, then serve and enjoy!

Chocolate Pumpkin Skeleton Cupcakes

Inspired by the King of Halloween, these chocolate pumpkin skeleton cupcakes are the perfect combination of trick and treat! From piping the black and white swirled buttercream to drawing the skeleton faces, you'll have lots of spooky fun making these.

MAKES 12

Cupcakes
- 125ml vegetable oil
- 180g golden caster sugar
- 2 medium eggs, room temperature
- 200g pumpkin purée
- 200g self-raising flour
- 1 tsp baking powder
- 50g cocoa powder
- 1½ tsp ground cinnamon or pumpkin spice

Buttercream
- 200g unsalted butter, room temperature
- 400g icing sugar
- 2 tbsp milk
- 1 tsp vanilla extract
- black food colouring

Decoration
- chocolate writing icing
- 12 white chocolate-coated biscuits

Preheat the oven to 180°C/160°C fan and line a 12-hole cupcake tin with 12 paper cases.

In a large bowl, whisk the vegetable oil, caster sugar and eggs together until well combined. Stir in the pumpkin purée.

In a separate bowl, add the flour, baking powder, cocoa powder and cinnamon or pumpkin spice and stir together. Add to the wet ingredients and fold together until the cake mixture is smooth and combined.

Divide the mixture evenly between the cases, filling each three-quarters full.

Bake for 20–22 minutes until risen and springy to the touch (a toothpick inserted into the middle should come out clean). Leave to cool completely on a wire rack.

To make the buttercream, beat the butter in a bowl until soft and pale in colour. Sift in the icing sugar, then add the milk and vanilla extract. Beat until the buttercream is smooth.

Divide the buttercream between two bowls and add a few drops of black food colouring to one bowl to make a black buttercream.

Fit a large piping bag with a closed-star nozzle. Spoon the white buttercream into one side of the piping bag, and the black buttercream into the other side. Twist the top

of the piping bag and push the buttercream down to the nozzle.

Pipe swirls of the two-tone buttercream on top of each cupcake. Use the chocolate writing icing to draw the skeleton faces onto the biscuits. Get creative and try out different expressions!

To finish, place a skeleton biscuit on top of each cupcake.

··

BAKING TIP
Save time by decorating the skeleton biscuits while the cupcakes are baking in the oven.

71

White Chocolate & Peppermint Gnome Cupcakes

With their chocolate snowball noses, snowy strawberry hats and festive flavour, these adorable cupcakes are bound to bring a touch of festive magic to your Christmas! The simple decoration also makes this an ideal recipe to get little helpers involved in the kitchen.

MAKES 12

Cupcakes
- 180g unsalted butter, room temperature
- 180g caster sugar
- 2 medium eggs, room temperature
- 180g self-raising flour
- 2 tbsp milk
- 100g white chocolate chips

Buttercream
- 100g white chocolate, chopped
- 200g salted butter, room temperature
- 350g icing sugar, plus extra to finish
- ½ tsp peppermint extract

Decoration
- 12 large strawberries
- 12 coated chocolate snowballs (I use Cadbury Mini SnowBalls)
- chocolate writing icing

Preheat the oven to 180°C/160°C fan and line a 12-hole cupcake tin with 12 paper cases. Cream the butter and caster sugar together in a large bowl until light and fluffy. Beat in the eggs one at a time. Then fold in the flour, milk and white chocolate chips.

Divide the mixture evenly between the paper cases, filling each one three-quarters full, then bake for 20–22 minutes until risen and springy to the touch. Leave to cool on a wire rack.

To make the buttercream, first melt the white chocolate in a heatproof bowl in the microwave for 30–60 seconds, or set over a pan of simmering water until melted.

In a separate bowl, beat the butter until soft and pale in colour. Sift in the icing sugar and add the peppermint extract. Beat well until smooth. Fold in the melted white chocolate, then spread or pipe the buttercream on top of the cupcakes.

To decorate, cut off the tops of the fresh strawberries and place upside down on top of the buttercream. Add a chocolate snowball to each cupcake for the gnome's nose and two small dots using the chocolate writing icing for the eyes. To finish, sift a dusting of icing sugar over the strawberry hats. Serve and enjoy!

Christmas Cheer Cupcakes

With a soft chocolate sponge, Grinchy green buttercream and tiny heart sprinkles, who could resist stealing a bite of these cupcakes? They're joyful, delicious and sure to bring you Christmas cheer (whether you like it or not!).

MAKES 12

Cupcakes
- 180g unsalted butter, room temperature
- 180g caster sugar
- 2 medium eggs, room temperature
- 150g self-raising flour
- 30g cocoa powder
- 2 tbsp milk

Buttercream
- 200g salted butter, room temperature
- 400g icing sugar
- 2 tbsp milk
- green food colouring

Decoration
- 50g mixed red and green chocolate beans (I used Christmas M&M's)
- heart-shaped sprinkles
- Christmas sprinkles

Preheat the oven to 180°C/160°C fan and line a 12-hole cupcake tin with 12 paper cases.

Cream the butter and caster sugar together in a large bowl until light and fluffy. Beat in the eggs one at a time. Fold in the flour, cocoa powder and milk to make a smooth chocolate cake mixture.

Divide the mixture evenly between the paper cases, filling each one three-quarters full.

Bake for 20–22 minutes until risen and springy to the touch. Leave to cool completely on a wire rack.

To make the buttercream, beat the butter until soft and pale in colour. Sift in the icing sugar and add the milk. Beat well until smooth. Mix in a few drops of green food colouring to dye the buttercream a Grinch-like green.

Fit a large piping bag with an open-star nozzle and fill with the green buttercream. Pipe tall swirls of buttercream on top of each cupcake.

Decorate using the chocolate beans and sprinkles, placing a heart sprinkle at the very top of each to add some Christmas cheer!

BAKING TIP
Swap the heart sprinkles for gold stars to turn these cupcakes into adorable Christmas trees.

Slabs &
Sharing Boards

Chocolate Eggs-presso Martinis

Pair these Chocolate Eggs-presso Martinis with your Easter brunch or dinner celebrations for a delicious sweet pick-me-up. Just mix the ingredients in a cocktail shaker, pour into hollow chocolate eggs and say 'cheers!'

MAKES 6

- 6 small foil-wrapped hollow chocolate eggs
- 50ml vodka
- 50ml coffee liqueur
- 50ml cold espresso coffee
- 2 tbsp chocolate sauce
- handful of ice cubes

Run a sharp knife under hot water for 20 seconds, then dry with kitchen paper.

Unwrap the chocolate eggs and carefully cut off the top of each. Stand upright in egg cups or shot glasses on a serving plate or board.

Add the vodka, coffee liqueur, espresso coffee, chocolate sauce and ice cubes to a cocktail shaker. Shake vigorously for 30 seconds.

Strain into a jug (this will make the pouring easier) and then pour the martini into the chocolate eggs, filling each one to the top.

Serve and sip!

Dippy Egg Cheesecake

Get ready to dip buttery shortbread soldiers into this creamy vanilla cheesecake with a lemon curd yolk! Served in a chocolate eggshell, this delicious dessert is perfect for sharing with friends and family after your Easter Sunday lunch.

SERVES 6+

Shortbread
- 200g unsalted butter, room temperature
- 100g caster sugar
- 300g plain flour
- 1 tsp ground cinnamon (optional)
- 1 tsp granulated sugar (optional)

Cheesecake
- 1 large hollow chocolate Easter egg
- 300g full-fat cream cheese
- 75g icing sugar
- 1 tsp vanilla extract
- 150ml double cream
- 2 tbsp lemon curd

....

BAKING TIP
To give the shortbread soldiers a toast-like appearance, stir some cinnamon and granulated sugar together and scatter on top once baked and cooled.

Preheat the oven to 200°C/180°C fan and line a 20cm square baking tin with greaseproof paper.

Start by making the shortbread soldiers. Cream the butter and caster sugar together in a large bowl until light and fluffy. Add the flour and use clean hands to bring the mixture together into a dough. Press the dough out in the baking tin and prick the top all over using a fork.

Bake for 20 minutes until golden around the edges. As soon as the shortbread is out of the oven, use a sharp knife to score seven lines down and one line across the centre (this will make the shortbread soldiers easier to cut once baked). Leave to cool completely.

Meanwhile, make the Dippy Egg Cheesecake. Run a sharp knife under hot water and dry with kitchen paper. Carefully score around the chocolate egg until it separates into two halves.

Use an electric mixer to beat the cream cheese, icing sugar and vanilla extract together in a bowl until smooth. Add the double cream and whisk for 1–2 minutes until thick.

Spoon and spread the cheesecake filling into the easter egg halves and spoon 1 tablespoon of the lemon curd on top of each half for the yolks. Chill in the fridge for 30 minutes to set.

Meanwhile, slice the baked shortbread into soldiers. To serve, place the egg halves on a pretty plate and arrange the shortbread soldiers around the outside. Time to get dipping!

81

Easter Bunny Slab

Celebrate Easter with this delicious white chocolate slab topped with chocolate bunnies and eggs. Perfect for using up any leftover goodies or to make as a lovely edible gift instead of a chocolate egg. It's almost too pretty to crack ... almost!

SERVES 10+

- 400g white chocolate, chopped
- malt (white and milk) chocolate bunnies (I use Mini Malteser Bunnies)
- mini chocolate eggs (I use Cadbury Mini Eggs)
- Easter sprinkles

Line a large flat baking sheet with some greaseproof paper.

Melt the white chocolate in a heatproof bowl in the microwave for 60–80 seconds until smooth, or set over a pan of simmering water until melted.

Pour onto the baking sheet and use the back of a spoon to spread the chocolate out into a large rectangular shape.

Decorate with the malt chocolate bunnies, mini chocolate eggs and Easter sprinkles, then chill in the fridge for at least 3 hours or until set.

Break into shards and enjoy!

Try this seasonal twist

Swap the Easter treats for red, blue and white chocolate beans and sprinkles for a delicious 4th July snack.

Chilli Chocolate Cauldron Fondue

Do you dare to try this spicy chocolate fondue? Brewed with just a hint of chilli, the fondue is rich, indulgent and perfect for sharing with friends while watching a scary movie. Serve in a traditional fondue pot or a black cauldron for added thrills, along with a selection of spooky dipping treats!

SERVES 6–8

Fondue
- 200g dark chocolate (70% cocoa solids), finely chopped
- 200g milk chocolate, finely chopped
- 400ml double cream
- 1 tsp mild chilli powder

Dipping Treats
- strawberry monsters
- pretzel bones
- marshmallow ghosts

Add the chopped dark and milk chocolates, the double cream and chilli powder to a heatproof bowl and microwave for 90 seconds. Leave to sit for 20 seconds, then stir until the chocolate fondue is smooth.

Pour into a fondue pot or black cauldron and place in the middle of a serving plate.

Arrange the spooky dipping treats around the outside and dip in straightaway!

BAKING TIP
Can't handle the heat? This recipe works just as well without the chilli powder.

Death By Chocolate Milkshake

Turn this thick and creamy Death By Chocolate Milkshake into the ultimate Halloween indulgence by adding your own topping treats! Choose from marshmallow ghosts, jelly worm sweets, crushed biscuits ... the options are endless and remember, when it comes to Halloween, more is more!

SERVES 2

Milkshake
- 300g chocolate fudge ice cream
- 300ml milk of your choice
- chocolate sauce, for drizzling

Topping Treats
- whipped cream
- chocolate sprinkles
- chocolates (I use peanut butter cups and chocolate beans)
- sweets (I use jelly worms and Candy Corns)
- biscuits (I use chocolate wafers and cookies & cream biscuits)

....

BAKING TIP
Turn up the thrill factor by stirring a measure of spiced rum into each milkshake.

Add the chocolate fudge ice cream and milk to a blender. Blend until smooth and thick.

Drizzle the chocolate sauce around the inside of two milkshake glasses, then pour in the chocolate milkshake.

Top with whipped cream, sprinkle over the chocolate sprinkles and serve with a selection of your favourite treats to decorate the milkshakes. Enjoy!

Spiderweb Chocolate Slab

Caught in a web of chocolate, peanut butter and edible spiders – this easy Spiderweb Chocolate Slab can be broken into shards for a frightfully delicious Halloween treat!

SERVES 10+

- 350g milk chocolate, chopped
- 50g white chocolate, chopped
- 12 liquorice strands
- 3 peanut butter cups (I use Reese's Peanut Butter Cups)
- 6 edible eyes
- 50g peanut butter chocolate beans (I use Reese's Pieces)

Line a large flat baking sheet with greaseproof paper and set aside.

Melt the milk chocolate in a heatproof bowl in the microwave for 60–80 seconds until smooth, or set over a pan of simmering water until melted. Set aside for now.

Melt the white chocolate in the same way, then transfer to a piping bag and snip off the tip to make a small hole.

Pour the melted milk chocolate onto the baking sheet and use a spoon to spread it out into a thin rectangular shape.

Pipe spirals of white chocolate on top, some big, some small. Drag a toothpick through the spirals to make a spiderweb pattern.

Slice each liquorice strand lengthways to make two thinner strands, giving 24 in total.

Place the peanut butter cups on top of the big spiderwebs, then arrange 8 liquorice strands around each cup for the spider legs. Dab the edible eyes with leftover chocolate and place two on top of each peanut butter cup.

Scatter over the peanut butter chocolate beans, then chill in the fridge for at least 3 hours or until set.

Break into shards and enjoy!

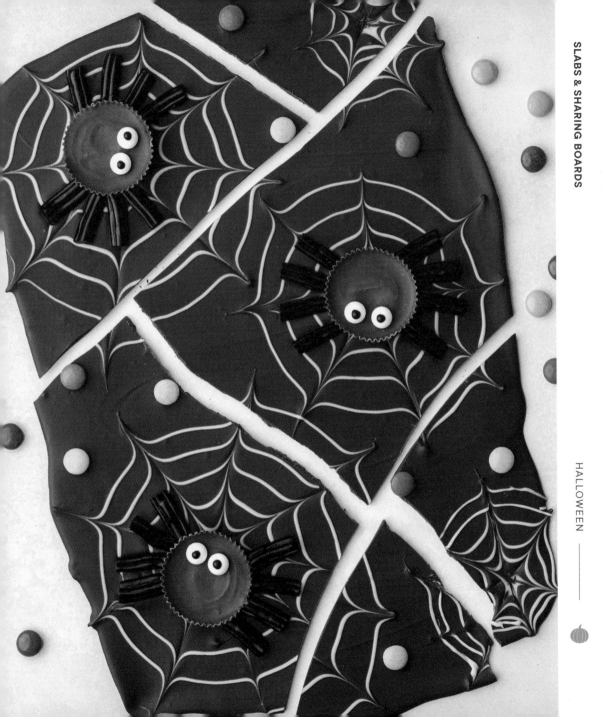

Elf's Breakfast Bark

This quick and easy Elf's Breakfast Bark is made using their four main food groups ... candy, candy, candy and more candy! Break the bark into shards, share with your buddies and spread some Christmas cheer with every bite.

SERVES 10+

- 300g milk chocolate, chopped
- 100g white chocolate, chopped
- candy canes
- pretzels, crushed
- green, red and white chocolate beans (I use Christmas M&M's)
- mini marshmallows
- Christmas sprinkles

Line a large flat baking sheet with some greaseproof paper.

Melt the milk chocolate in a heatproof bowl in the microwave for 60–80 seconds until smooth, or set over a pan of simmering water, until melted. Set aside for now.

Melt the white chocolate in the same way as the milk chocolate above.

Pour the melted milk chocolate onto the baking sheet and use a spoon to spread it out into a thin rectangular shape.

Drizzle the white chocolate on top, then use a toothpick to create a swirly pattern.

Scatter over the candy canes, crushed pretzels, chocolate beans, mini marshmallows and Christmas sprinkles.

Chill in the fridge for at least 3 hours or until set, then break into shards and enjoy!

Salted Caramel Hot Chocolate Topping Board

This Salted Caramel Hot Chocolate Topping Board is a wonderful experience to enjoy with friends and family – did someone say Christmas movie?! For the hot chocolate, you can use any milk you like and if you fancy a tipple, add a measure of Irish cream liqueur, too.

SERVES 4

Hot Chocolate
- 120g salted caramel dark chocolate, finely chopped
- 1 litre milk of your choice

Topping Board Treats
- mini marshmallows
- candy canes
- Christmas sprinkles
- green, red and white chocolate beans (I use Christmas M&M's)
- cinnamon sticks
- salted caramel sauce
- whipped cream
- chocolate flake bars
- peppermint candies
- malt chocolate reindeer (I use Mini Malteser Reindeer)
- milk chocolate drops (I use Hershey's)
- coated chocolate snowballs (I use Cadbury Mini Snow Balls)

Put the salted caramel dark chocolate into a large heatproof jug.

Heat the milk in a pan over a low heat until piping hot and steaming.

Pour the hot milk into the jug and leave to sit for 30 seconds. Then give it a stir until all the chocolate has melted.

Pour the hot chocolate into four festive mugs (if using Irish Cream liqueur, stir 25ml into each mug at this stage).

Arrange the mugs of hot chocolate on a large wooden board along with your selection of topping treats.

Chocolate Ice Cream Sundae Bar

Made for sharing with friends or family, this Chocolate Ice Cream Sundae Bar is the perfect sweet buffet to accompany your Christmas movie night. Grab a bowl and dig in!

SERVES 4

Ice Cream
- 397g tin sweetened condensed milk
- 50g cocoa powder
- 600ml double cream
- 200g dark chocolate chips

Sundae Bar Treats
- waffle cones
- wafer biscuits
- peppermint candies
- candy canes
- Christmas sprinkles
- chocolate beans (I use M&M's)
- mini marshmallows

Pour the condensed milk into a bowl and sift in the cocoa powder. Stir to combine.

In a separate bowl, use an electric mixer to whip the cream on high speed until it holds stiff peaks. This will take 3–5 minutes.

Pour the condensed milk and cocoa mixture into the whipped cream and add the chocolate chips. Fold until combined.

Add the mixture to a 900g loaf tin, spreading it out evenly. Cover with foil and freeze for at least 6 hours or overnight.

Place a large ice-cream sundae glass in the freezer an hour before serving. Meanwhile, start arranging the sundae bar treats on a serving board.

Remove the chocolate chip ice cream from the freezer and leave to soften for 10 minutes. Then scoop the ice cream into the chilled glass and place in the middle of the board. Serve with bowls and spoons!

Index

blondies
  lemon & white chocolate bunny
    blondies 12
  red velvet Santa hat blondies 22
  trick-or-treat blondie bars 18
brownies
  bubbling cauldron brownies 14
  cosmic bat brownies 16–17
  dozen egg brownies 8
  hot cross bun brownies 11
  Rudolph brownies 21
  snowball brownies 24

cakes
  carrot patch cake 28
  chocolate orange wreath cake 38
  Christmas cheer cupcakes 74
  cracked egg chocolate cupcakes
    67
  Easter nest cupcakes 65
  Halloween party cake 36–7
  hot cross mug cake 32
  monster mash loaf cake 35
  Rudolph malted chocolate mug
    cake 40
  skeleton cupcakes 70–1
  white chocolate & peppermint
    gnome cupcakes 72
  wicked witch cupcakes 68
caramel
  salted caramel egg cookies 46
  salted caramel hot chocolate
    topping board 90
carrot patch cake 28
cheesecakes
  dippy egg cheesecake 81
chocolate beans
  chocolate ice cream sundae bar
    92
  Christmas cheer cupcakes 74
  cookies for Santa 56
  elf's breakfast bark 89

Halloween party cake 36–7
maple mummy cookies 53
Rudolph brownies 21
salted caramel hot chocolate
  topping board 90
spiderweb chocolate slab 86
trick-or-treat blondie bars 18
wicked witch cupcakes 68
chocolate buttons
  s'mores spiderweb cookies 55
chocolate drops
  salted caramel hot chocolate
    topping board 90
  wicked witch cupcakes 68
chocolate eggs
  bubbling cauldron brownies 14
  bunny hug biscuits 45
  chocolate eggs-presso martinis
    78
  chocolate simnel cake 30–1
  cracked egg chocolate cupcakes
    67
  dozen egg brownies 8
  Easter bunny slab 82
  Easter nest cupcakes 65
  egg hunt cookie bars 48
  hot cross mug cake 32
  salted caramel egg cookies 46
chocolate hazelnut spread
  Linzer love cookies, actually 59
chocolate orange segments
  chocolate orange wreath cake
    38
chocolate snowballs
  red velvet Santa hat blondies 22
  snowball brownies 24
  white chocolate & peppermint
    gnome cupcakes 72
chocolate sticks
  bubbling cauldron brownies 14
  snowman puddle peanut butter
    cookies 60

Christmas
  chocolate ice cream sundae bar
    92
  chocolate orange wreath cake 38
  Christmas cheer cupcakes 74
  cookies for Santa 56
  elf's breakfast bark 89
  Linzer love cookies, actually 59
  red velvet Santa hat blondies 22
  Rudolph brownies 21
  Rudolph malted chocolate mug
    cake 40
  salted caramel hot chocolate
    topping board 90
  snowball brownies 24
  snowman puddle peanut butter
    cookies 60
  white chocolate & peppermint
    gnome cupcakes 72
coffee
  chocolate eggs-presso martinis
    78
cookies & biscuits
  bunny hug biscuits 45
  cookies & scream bars 50
  cookies for Santa 56
  egg hunt cookie bars 48
  Linzer love cookies, actually 59
  maple mummy cookies 53
  salted caramel egg cookies 46
  s'mores spiderweb cookies 55
  snowman puddle peanut butter
    cookies 60
cream
  chilli chocolate cauldron fondue
    84
  chocolate ice cream sundae bar
    92
  chocolate orange wreath cake 38
  chocolate simnel cake 30–1
  cosmic bat brownies 16–17
  death by chocolate milkshake 85

dippy egg cheesecake 81
Rudolph malted chocolate mug cake 40
salted caramel hot chocolate topping board 90

cream cheese
carrot patch cake 28
dippy egg cheesecake 81

dark chocolate
bubbling cauldron brownies 14
chilli chocolate cauldron fondue 84
chocolate ice cream sundae bar 92
chocolate orange wreath cake 38
chocolate simnel cake 30–1
cosmic bat brownies 16–17
dozen egg brownies 8
hot cross bun brownies 11
Rudolph brownies 21
salted caramel egg cookies 46
salted caramel hot chocolate topping board 90
snowball brownies 24

Easter
bunny hug biscuits 45
carrot patch cake 28
chocolate eggs-presso martinis 78
chocolate simnel cake 30–1
cracked egg chocolate cupcakes 67
dippy egg cheesecake 81
dozen egg brownies 8
Easter bunny slab 82
Easter nest cupcakes 65
egg hunt cookie bars 48
hot cross bun brownies 11
hot cross mug cake 32
lemon & white chocolate bunny blondies 12
salted caramel egg cookies 46

Halloween
bubbling cauldron brownies 14

chilli chocolate cauldron fondue 84
cookies & scream bars 50
cosmic bat brownies 16–17
death by chocolate milkshake 85
Halloween party cake 36–7
maple mummy cookies 53
monster mash loaf cake 35
skeleton cupcakes 70–1
s'mores spiderweb cookies 55
spiderweb chocolate slab 86
trick-or-treat blondie bars 18
wicked witch cupcakes 68

ice cream
chocolate ice cream sundae bar 92
death by chocolate milkshake 85
Independence Day
Easter bunny slab (variation) 82

malted chocolate
Easter bunny slab 82
Rudolph malted chocolate mug cake 40
marshmallows
chilli chocolate cauldron fondue 84
chocolate ice cream sundae bar 92
elf's breakfast bark 89
salted caramel hot chocolate topping board 90
s'mores spiderweb cookies 55
snowman puddle peanut butter cookies 60
milk
death by chocolate milkshake 85
salted caramel hot chocolate topping board 90
milk chocolate
chilli chocolate cauldron fondue 84
cosmic bat brownies 16–17
elf's breakfast bark 89
spiderweb chocolate slab 86
Mother's Day
carrot patch cake (variation) 28

peanut butter
snowman puddle peanut butter cookies 60
peanut butter chocolates
snowman puddle peanut butter cookies 60
spiderweb chocolate slab 86
wicked witch cupcakes 68
pumpkin
skeleton cupcakes 70–1

shortbread
dippy egg cheesecake 81

Thanksgiving Day
cookies & scream bars (variation) 50
toppings, various
chocolate ice cream sundae bar 92
death by chocolate milkshake 85
Rudolph malted chocolate mug cake 40
salted caramel hot chocolate topping board 90

vodka
chocolate eggs-presso martinis 78

white chocolate
carrot patch cake 28
Easter bunny slab 82
Easter nest cupcakes 65
elf's breakfast bark 89
Halloween party cake 36–7
hot cross bun brownies 11
lemon & white chocolate bunny blondies 12
maple mummy cookies 53
red velvet Santa hat blondies 22
snowman puddle peanut butter cookies 60
spiderweb chocolate slab 86
white chocolate & peppermint gnome cupcakes 72

About the Author

Jessica Marsden-Urquhart, known to most as Jessie Bakes Cakes, is a self-taught baker, recipe developer and digital content creator, on a mission to spread joy through baking. Her passion for all things sweet (especially chocolate!) shines through her delicious recipes that celebrate the seasons both in appearance and flavour.

Jessie hopes to inspire bakers of all skill levels to embrace their creativity in the kitchen, enjoy baking up a storm, and share the sweetness with their friends and family. After all, happiness is a piece of cake!

Acknowledgements

I'll start by thanking the person who has been there throughout my entire baking journey and the making of this book – my incredible husband Sam (aka chief taste tester and number one fan). I'm so grateful for your endless words of encouragement and reassurance whenever my imposter syndrome kicked in and I cannot put into words how much you mean to me.

To my gorgeous family and friends for being superstar cheerleaders and for always asking "so how's the book coming along!?". Your genuine excitement, interest and support kept me going through all the late nights and weekends spent working. Can't thank you enough!

Now to my amazing online baking community who have helped shape this book and made it possible without even knowing. Keeping it a secret from you has been so challenging, but now it's out in the wild, I cannot wait to hear what you think and see your *Chocolate Overload* creations!

Special mention to Denby Pottery who supplied the stunning crockery and Capture by Lucy for your fabulous backdrops that feature in all the photographs.

Finally, thank you to the whole team at Penguin who have guided me through this process and been a pleasure to work with. Especially, Lucie and Laura for your patience with my endless questions and last-minute changes. Your expertise and creativity have been invaluable to the making of this book.